AMERICAN INDIAN LIFE

The Sioux
The Past and Present of the Dakota, Lakota, and Nakota

by Donna Janell Bowman

Consultant:
Brett Barker, PhD
Associate Professor of History
University of Wisconsin–Marathon County

CAPSTONE PRESS
a capstone imprint

Fact Finders Books are published by Capstone Press,
1710 Roe Crest Drive, North Mankato, Minnesota 56003
www.capstonepub.com

Library of Congress Cataloging-in-Publication Data
Bowman, Donna Janell.
  The Sioux : the past and present of the Dakota, Lakota, and Nakota /
by Donna Janell Bowman.
pages cm.—(Fact finders. American Indian life)
Includes bibliographical references and index.
Audience: Grades 4-6.
ISBN 978-1-4914-4990-5 (library binding)
ISBN 978-1-4914-5002-4 (paperback)
ISBN 978-1-4914-5006-2 (ebook pdf)
1. Dakota Indians—History—Juvenile literature. I. Title.
E99.D1B78 2015
978.004'9752—dc23   2015009402

Editorial Credits
Catherine Neitge, editor; Tracy Davies McCabe, designer;
Svetlana Zhurkin, media researcher; Kathy McColley, production specialist

Source Notes
Page 15, line 1: *Through Indian Eyes: The Untold Story of Native American
Peoples*. Pleasantville, N.Y.: Reader's Digest Association, 1995, p. 318.

Photo Credits
Alamy: Haytham Pictures, cover (bottom right); Corbis, 24; Dreamstime: Joe
Ferrer, 27, 29; Getty Images: Print Collector/Art Media, 15, Rick Rudnicki,
25, *The Washington Post*/Nikki Kahn, 16; Library of Congress, 12; National
Geographic Creative: Aaron Huey, 20, 21; Newscom: Danita Delimont
Photography/Angel Wynn, 28, Danita Delimont Photography/Cindy Miller
Hopkins, 22 (right), 26; North Wind Picture Archives, 11, NativeStock,
5 (bottom), 18, 22 (left); Shutterstock: Dennis W. Donohue, 5 (top),
Marzolino, cover (top), 1, Wollertz, cover (bottom left), 19; SuperStock, 9,
age fotostock/Jim West, 23, Newberry Library, 6; XNR Productions, 17

Printed in Canada.
032015   008825FRF15

Table of Contents

Celebrating with Dance

Just outside a large circular area, drummers bang a large rawhide drum. Their drumbeats are strong and rhythmic, like the heartbeat of their ancestors. The ground has already been blessed. It is their way of thanking the Creator for another wacipi—a powwow. While the drummers drum, they sing in their native language. They sing **vocables** too—powerful sounds that express emotion.

A man carries an eagle feather staff into the arena. It represents the native people. Behind him an honor guard of Sioux military veterans carries American, state, tribal, and veterans' flags. The Grand Entry has begun.

Hundreds of dancers from the Great Sioux Nation stream into the arena. Each one dances in step with the drum. Powwows are a time for Sioux and other native tribes to gather and celebrate life. It is a time to reconnect with friends and to honor their rich culture.

vocable: word made up of sounds without regard to meaning

EAGLE FEATHERS

The eagle is the most loved animal of the Great Spirit, according to American Indian legend. It is the bravest and strongest of all birds. Eagles and their feathers have long been considered sacred. The dark and light feathers represent daylight and darkness, summer and winter, peace and war, life and death. Throughout history eagle feathers have been awarded for acts of bravery.

Grand Entry during a powwow on the Pine Ridge Reservation

Chapter 1

Early Days

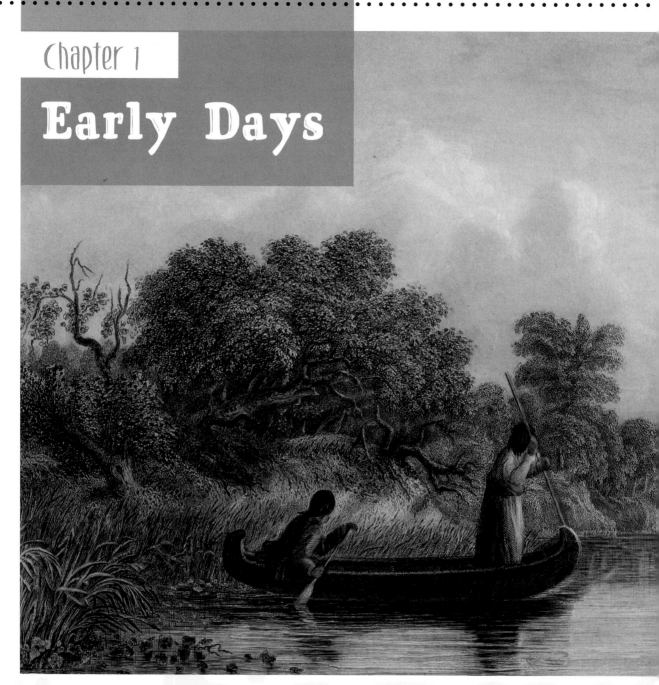

Artist and Army officer Seth Eastman painted Dakota spear fishing from a canoe in the mid-1800s.

The ancestors of today's Sioux lived in the woodlands near the Great Lakes. They hunted and fished and gathered wild rice. War with the Ojibwe in the 1600s pushed the Sioux south and west. They settled in present-day southern Minnesota, North Dakota, and South Dakota.

Seven separate but close-knit Sioux **bands** formed an **alliance** of three tribes—the Dakota, Nakota, and Lakota. Their similar cultures and beliefs made them perfect allies. They were the Oceti Sakowin—the Seven Council Fires.

Tribal name

Members of an enemy tribe, the Ojibwe, were responsible for the Sioux name. They called the tribe the *na-towe-ssiwa*. It meant "people of a different tribe" or "snakes" in the Ojibwe language. French fur traders mispronounced it in the 1600s and shortened it to Sioux. The Sioux prefer to be called Dakota, Nakota, or Lakota, which mean "the people."

band: group of related people who live and hunt together
alliance: agreement between groups to work together

DAKOTA

The Dakota lived a woodland lifestyle, mostly in Minnesota and Wisconsin. They lived in small villages. They grew corn, beans, and squash, which are called the three sisters. They grow well together. The men hunted and fished. Families gathered wild rice from rivers and lakes. In winter they lived off supplies saved during previous months. In spring men left on hunting parties and everyone else in the village moved into sugaring camps. It is where they gathered to make sugar and syrup from maple trees. All food was shared among the village.

LAKOTA AND NAKOTA

The largest Sioux tribe, the Lakota, migrated west of the Missouri River, around the sacred Black Hills. To the Lakota the Black Hills are Paha Sapa, "The Heart of Everything That Is." They believe it was the sacred place of creation.

The Nakota, the smallest tribe of Sioux, settled in the middle part of Sioux territory. They lived along the James River, mostly in the prairies of eastern North Dakota and South Dakota. They hunted and grew crops.

The Lakota were the most nomadic tribe. They roamed the plains of the Dakotas, Wyoming, Nebraska, and Montana. They traded with other Plains Indians for horses and owned large herds.

sacred: holy

nomadic: traveling from place to place according to the seasons in search of food and water

THE BUFFALO

The Lakota and some Nakota followed the migration of the buffalo, which were key to the bands' survival. The buffalo provided almost everything the Lakota and Nakota needed. Buffalo hides were made into clothing, blankets, and homes. The skins were used to make moccasin soles, drums, shields, and bags. Buffalo bones were carved into tools and needles for sewing. Horns were made into cups and spoons.

Each buffalo provided hundreds of pounds of meat. The bands enjoyed fresh meat after a hunt. The women dried the rest of the meat for later use.

Buffalo hunts were dangerous. The largest buffalo stood 6 feet (183 centimeters) tall and weighed 1 ton (907 kilograms). Before the Sioux had horses, they hunted buffalo on foot. It was exhausting and not very productive. After they acquired horses, hunters rode beside the running herd and shot the buffalo with bows and arrows. Women followed behind and cut up the dead animals for meat and hides.

Buffalo were important to Sioux survival.

9

FAMILY LIFE

The Sioux lived in camps or villages, depending on the band's location and the time of year. The Dakota in Minnesota and Wisconsin lived in bark-covered wooden houses.

The Sioux on the Plains lived in cone-shaped tents called tepees. It is also spelled tipi. The word comes from the Dakota language. Three heavy poles tied with rope formed a cone shape. Depending on its size, as many as 18 smaller poles were used to form the frame. Buffalo hide was stretched across the frame and anchored to the ground. Most tepees used about 16 hides, which were sewn together.

Sioux life revolved around family. All people in a camp were related by birth, marriage, or adoption. The large groups were called bands. Men spent much of the year hunting to provide food for the bands. They also raided enemy tribes for horses. The animals had been brought to North America by the Spanish. Horses reached the Plains by the early 1700s. Owning horses was a sign of wealth. The Sioux gave horses as gifts, traded them for guns, and trained them for battle.

Women cooked and handled other duties around the camp. They also gathered wild fruits and vegetables. In some bands they raised crops.

Women spent many hours tanning fresh buffalo hides to make clothing and tepee covers. Most men wore breechcloths in warm weather and buckskin shirts and leggings in cold weather. Women wore buckskin dresses and leggings. They decorated their clothing with porcupine quills and beads.

Buffalo meat drying in the sun

Children were at the center of attention. Grandparents took charge of the youngest children, the *wakanisha*. Girls worked alongside their mothers and learned to sew, cook, and gather wild plants. Boys learned to ride horses at an early age and often tended to the herds.

In late spring or early summer the Sioux bands came together to trade, hunt buffalo, race horses, and meet with band leaders. They visited their friends, ate meals together, and danced. Young people met possible future marriage partners. The Sioux from the west traded horses and buffalo hides to the Dakota for metal pots, knives, axes, and guns. The Dakota had acquired the items trading with Europeans farther east.

Chapter 2

Broken Treaties

Battles between Minnesota settlers and the Dakota in 1862 resulted in many deaths.

The United States was eager to expand by the 1800s. Settlers and prospectors flocked west in search of gold and farmland. As they disrupted the American Indians' way of life the Sioux and other tribes fought back.

A long series of **treaties** between the United States and various tribes began. The Sioux and other tribes gave up land and agreed not to bother travelers. In return, they were promised their own land, money, and food. But as more settlers moved in, the U.S. government broke its treaty promises.

The Dakota, along with other tribes, signed the Treaty of Traverse des Sioux in 1851. It gave up most of their land in Minnesota. The Dakota were moved to **reservations** in Minnesota, North and South Dakota, Nebraska, and Montana. They were promised food, supplies, and money. But during the Civil War, the U.S. government fell behind on its payments. The Dakota were starving and angry. They clashed with settlers in southern Minnesota. The conflict turned into a full-scale war, with hundreds dead on each side. After their defeat in late 1862, more than 300 Dakota men were sentenced to death. Most were saved by the order of President Abraham Lincoln, but 38 were hanged.

treaty: an official agreement between two or more groups or countries

reservation: area of land set aside by the government for American Indians; in Canada reservations are called reserves

13

RED CLOUD'S WAR

The Lakota also faced loss of their land. The discovery of gold brought thousands of prospectors to the Plains. U.S. forces came west to open a road through the best Lakota hunting grounds in 1866. Lakota warrior and statesman Red Cloud responded. For two years he led a war on soldiers and civilians in Wyoming. He demanded that the road be closed and that military forts be destroyed. Red Cloud won. The result was the Treaty of Fort Laramie in 1868. It protected Lakota land from South Dakota into Montana. And the sacred Black Hills were promised to the Lakota forever. They were part of the Great Sioux Reservation created by the treaty.

Red Cloud believed he was protecting the Lakota way of life by agreeing to live on the huge reservation. But not all Lakota leaders, including Sitting Bull and Crazy Horse, were in favor of the new way of life. They wanted to continue to live as they had for years.

After gold was discovered in the Black Hills miners streamed onto Lakota land. The government allowed them into the Black Hills, in direct violation of the Treaty of Fort Laramie. The Lakota refused to accept the miners in their sacred place. President Ulysses S. Grant ordered all Sioux to move to reservation lands. Sitting Bull and Crazy Horse and their followers refused Grant's order.

prospector: person who looks for valuable minerals, especially silver and gold

Amos Bad Heart Bull, a Lakota, drew Custer's soldiers trying to escape.

As Crazy Horse said, "We did not ask you white men to come here. We do not want your civilization—we would live as our fathers did, and their fathers before them."

The president ordered the army to destroy their camps. The Lakota then allied with the Cheyenne and Arapaho in a final battle—the Battle of the Little Bighorn. The Indians defeated Lieutenant Colonel George Custer and the 7th Cavalry. But it didn't stop the army from tracking them down. They starved the Lakota. They destroyed Lakota camps and killed buffalo. By spring 1877 most Lakota were living on the reservation. Life was difficult.

Chapter 3

Sioux Life Today

Two young men ride horses on the vast Pine Ridge Reservation.

Today the Great Sioux Nation has about 170,000 members. About half live on or near reservations or communities in North Dakota, South Dakota, Minnesota, Montana, and Nebraska. About one-third of the members live in urban areas. The Sioux make up one of the largest groups of American Indians in the United States.

BUFFALO ARE BACK

Buffalo once again roam the Plains, but it wasn't always the case. The U.S. government knew the Lakota could not survive their traditional way of life without the buffalo. In the 1870s the army began sponsoring buffalo hunts from open trains. Buffalo were killed for sport and for their tongues and hides. The huge animals were left to rot where they fell. By 1884 only 325 buffalo were left on the Plains, where there had been thousands. Today buffalo have recovered from near extinction and number about 500,000.

The three Sioux tribes are divided into bands. Four bands make up the Dakota. They are the Mdewakanton, Wahpekute, Sisseton, and Wahpeton. Two bands make up the Nakota. They are the Yankton and the Yanktonai.

There are seven Lakota bands, which make up the largest tribe. They are the Oglala, Sicanga (Brulé), Miniconjou, Hunkpapa, Sans Arc, Oohenump, and Sihasapa.

There are also about 1,500 Dakota and Lakota who live on reserves in Canada. The Dakota there are descendants of those who escaped from Minnesota during the Dakota Conflict in 1862. The Lakota are descendants of Sitting Bull's Hunkpapa band who escaped to Canada after the Battle of the Little Bighorn.

Reservations are located in five states and two provinces.

TRIBAL GOVERNMENT

American Indians in the United States became citizens in 1924. Ten years later the Indian Reorganization Act was instituted. Tribes were encouraged to create their own constitutions and leadership.

Today each Sioux reservation or community has its own government. Elected tribal councils and delegates represent the residents. The councils meet regularly to discuss the needs of their communities. They manage the tribe's property and handle businesses to improve the tribe's economy. The tribal council represents the tribe in negotiations with the federal or state governments. A tribal court handles civil and criminal cases.

The Lower Brulé Sioux Tribe's colorful administration building

THE BLACK HILLS

The Blacks Hills are sacred to the Great Sioux Nation.

The Treaty of Fort Laramie promised the sacred Black Hills to the Sioux forever. But the United States broke the treaty and took the land. In 1980 the U.S. Supreme Court ordered the government to pay for land it took from the Lakota 100 years earlier. The government was ordered to pay $106 million to the Great Sioux Nation. That is the amount it owed in 1877 plus interest. The Sioux have refused to claim the funds, which have grown to more than $1 billion. They say the sacred Black Hills are not for sale.

They do not want the money. They want the Black Hills. Some Sioux admit it is nearly impossible to make everyone move from the Black Hills. One proposal would return more than 1 million acres (405,000 hectares) of land to them. The plan would also pay the tribes the money ordered by the Supreme Court plus millions of dollars in the future. The money would be considered rent on Sioux land, not payment for the sale of the land. The U.S. Congress would have to agree to a plan. So far it has not.

Chapter 4
Honoring the Past

The Sioux honor their **traditions** by teaching their language and culture to their children. Many Sioux children attend school on or near a reservation. Reservation schools teach students the Lakota, Dakota, and Nakota languages. After high school some teens choose to go to college near their homes. Several colleges are located on reservations. They include Sitting Bull College in North Dakota and Sinte Gleska University, Oglala Lakota College, and Sisseton Wahpeton College in South Dakota.

A Lakota language class sets up a tepee at Red Cloud Indian School on the Pine Ridge Reservation.

WORK

Many Sioux work away from the reservation. They are involved in many fields including medicine, the law, entertainment, and science. On the reservations people find jobs in casinos, shops, schools, and other businesses. Cattle ranching and farming are common occupations. Some Sioux ranchers raise buffalo.

An Oglala Lakota rides on his family's land in South Dakota.

tradition: custom, idea, or belief passed down through time

HANDCRAFTS

The Sioux are well known for their artistic skills. Many artists carry on traditional art forms such as beading and painting. For centuries the Sioux decorated clothing, blankets, saddles, and other items with handmade beads, shells, claws, bone, and porcupine quills. When Europeans brought beads to trade, the Sioux also began working with glass beads. Their distinct designs include geometric shapes, triangles, and symbols of Sioux life. A common color sequence was blue, yellow, red, and green, with a white background.

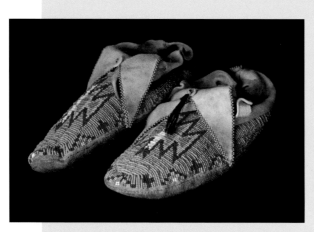

Traditional Sioux beadwork

Designs are painted on pottery made from red clay.

Painting images on buffalo robes, dresses, and hide shirts is a tradition that Sioux continue today. As their **ancestors** did, artists choose images that tell the story of Sioux life, including acts of bravery, and sacred symbols.

Long ago Sioux made pottery to hold food, water, and goods. Today traditional Sioux pottery is still made from the red clay of the Black Hills. It is decorated with important cultural symbols. The pottery is very popular with tourists and collectors.

Winter counts

Drawings and paintings on buffalo hide survive from the 1800s. They are called winter counts. They show important events in Sioux history.

ancestor: family member who lived a long time ago

SPORTS

Sioux youth participate in a wide range of sports and games. Lacrosse is one of the most popular. American Indians originated it centuries ago. At that time each tribe had its own name for the game. The Dakota called it Little Brother of War. The game was often used to settle territorial disputes between tribes, to vent aggression, and to practice for battle. Rules for the game have changed, but it is still a Sioux favorite.

BILLY MILLS WINS GOLD

Billy Mills is a famous Lakota athlete. He was born in 1938 and grew up on the Pine Ridge Reservation in South Dakota. He was orphaned at age 12. He turned his energy toward running and college. He was a star athlete at the University of Kansas.

Mills made history when he became the only American to win Olympic gold in the 10,000-meter race. He won his medal in the Summer Games in Tokyo, Japan, in 1964.

Mills co-founded and serves as spokesman for Running Strong for American Indian Youth. It supports cultural programs and provides health and housing assistance to American Indian communities.

President Barack Obama presented Mills with the 2012 Presidential Citizen's Medal. The 1983 movie *Running Brave* tells Mills' story.

FOOD

Sharing food with friends and family has always been an important part of Sioux life. Many of the foods prepared in the past are still made today. *Wojapi* is a traditional Lakota berry soup. Lakota plum cakes are also popular. *Wasna* is a traditional dish made from ground up dried buffalo, berries, and buffalo fat. It is also called pemmican. It is often used in ceremonies and rituals. *Wohanpi* is a traditional soup made with buffalo, potatoes, and carrots. Fry bread is a very popular food.

Buffalo meat is slowly dried to make pemmican.

MEDICINE

Many Sioux still turn to medicine men and women when they need physical or mental help. Medicine people know the sacred ceremonies. They experience spiritual visions and learn healing skills from **elders.** Their medicine bags hold medicinal herbs and plants. Sioux also visit medical centers and clinics on or near tribal lands. The U.S. Indian Health Service is responsible for providing many health services to American Indians.

elder: older person whose experience makes him or her a leader

RELIGION

The Sioux have always lived by four important virtues. They are wisdom, bravery, fortitude, and generosity. Giving gifts is a way to show friendship. Helping others is very important. Through songs, dances, prayers, and ceremonies, they honor the universe and spirits.

Sun Dance site in the Black Hills

The Sioux still honor their cultural religious traditions. They believe the Great Spirit, sometimes called the Great Mystery, created the world. Sky, earth, animals, and people are all related to each other and are dependent on each other for life. Spirits are in the sun, wind, rain, earth, animals, and plants.

They have always respected and honored everything that nature provided. Smoke from sacred pipes carries their prayers to the Great Spirit.

In the past when bands came together in early summer, they always held a Sun Dance ceremony. It lasted several days. The first days were spent in preparation. A pole was placed at the center of a dance circle. Men hung pieces of hide cut into the shapes of a man and a buffalo. They shot arrows at the cutouts while praying for success in hunting and war.

On the final day several men would perform a special ceremony to ask the spirits to protect the Sioux people. The men tied rawhide strips from the pole onto sharp bones. They shoved the bones through the skin of their chests and leaned back from the pole, pulling the strips tight. As they prayed they continued leaning back until the bones tore through the skin and they dropped to the ground. They believed their pain showed the spirits how much they were willing to suffer for their people. Today's Sun Dance is intended to renew people's relationship with the land. It includes skin piercings, dances, and prayers.

Reservations are also home to various Catholic and Protestant churches and schools.

Pipestone

Many Indian tribes use a unique red stone called pipestone for their sacred pipes. Only American Indians are allowed to take the stone from a quarry in southwestern Minnesota.

POWWOWS

Life isn't easy on Sioux reservations. They are among the poorest communities in the country. Many people do not have jobs. But the Sioux communities are working hard to make their lives better. An important way to celebrate their lives is with powwows.

Powwows are often competitions with prizes. Drumming and singing fill the air. Male traditional dancers dance stories of warriors and hunters. A bustle of feathers and a breastplate of claws or porcupine quills highlight their regalia. Female traditional dancers wear long buckskin or cloth dresses. They might carry a feathered fan or have a shawl draped over their arms.

Grass dancers, fancy dancers, and jingle dancers add to the excitement. As powwow spectators watch with wonder, the Sioux dance the stories of their people. They celebrate their strong ties to the past and present.

regalia: special clothes and decorations for ceremonies and celebrations

TIMELINE

1825: A treaty with the U.S. government confirms Sioux possession of lands ranging from Wisconsin to Wyoming.

1862: Dakota Conflict in Minnesota results in many deaths on both sides.

1868: The Treaty of Fort Laramie establishes the Great Sioux Reservation and promises to protect the sacred Black Hills and other Lakota lands from white invasion.

1874: Lieutenant Colonel George A. Custer leads an expedition into the Black Hills, where they discover gold. The next year the U.S. government offers the Lakota $6 million for rights to the Black Hills. The Lakota refuse.

1876: Lakota chief Sitting Bull leads Lakota, Northern Cheyenne, and Arapaho warriors against Custer and his 7th Cavalry on June 25 and 26 at the Battle of the Little Bighorn in Montana. Custer and more than 200 of his men were killed, a defeat that shocked the nation.

1881: Sitting Bull and his band surrender in North Dakota. All Sioux now live on reservations.

1890: Sitting Bull is killed. Army troops massacre more than 300 of Big Foot's band at Wounded Knee Creek on December 29.

1973: American Indian Movement protesters and their supporters take over the town of Wounded Knee, South Dakota, on February 27, starting a 71-day occupation. Most of the 1,200 people arrested and charged with crimes were acquitted.

1980: The U.S. Supreme Court orders the government to pay the Great Sioux Nation $102 million as compensation for taking the Black Hills. The Sioux refuse to accept the offer, which is now worth more than $1 billion.

1990: Congress apologizes to the descendants of those killed or wounded at the Wounded Knee massacre.

2009: President Barack Obama signs bill that includes text apologizing to American Indians for "many instances of violence, maltreatment, and neglect."

GLOSSARY

alliance (uh-LY-uhns)—agreement between groups to work together

ancestor (AN-sess-tur)—family member who lived a long time ago

band (BAND)—group of related people who live and hunt together

descendant (di-SEN-duhnt)—person who comes from a particular group of ancestors

elder (EL-dur)—older person whose experience makes him or her a leader

extinction (ik-STINGKT-shun)—the act of making extinct; an extinct animal is one that has died out, with no more of its kind

nomadic (noh-MAD-ik)—traveling from place to place according to the seasons in search of food and water

prospector (PROSS-pekt-or)—person who looks for valuable minerals, especially silver and gold

regalia (ri-GALE-yuh)—special clothes and decorations for ceremonies and celebrations

reservation (rez-er-VAY-shuhn)—area of land set aside by the government for American Indians; in Canada reservations are called reserves

sacred (SAY-krid)—holy

tradition (truh-DISH-uhn)—custom, idea, or belief passed down through time

treaty (TREE-tee)—an official agreement between two or more groups or countries

vocable (VOHK-uble)—word made up of sounds without regard to meaning

READ MORE

Collins, Terry. *Into the West: Causes and Effects of U.S. Westward Expansion*. North Mankato, Minn.: Capstone, 2014.

Higgins, Nadia. *Last Stand: Causes and Effects of the Battle of the Little Bighorn*. North Mankato, Minn.: Capstone, 2015.

McLaughlin, Timothy P., ed. *Walking on Earth and Touching the Sky: Poetry and Prose by Lakota Youth at Red Cloud Indian School*. New York: Abrams Books for Young Readers, 2012.

Zimmerman, Dwight Jon. *Saga of the Sioux: An Adaptation from Dee Brown's Bury My Heart at Wounded Knee*. New York: Henry Holt, 2011.

INTERNET SITES

FactHound offers a safe, fun way to find Internet sites related to this book. All of the sites on FactHound have been researched by our staff.

Here's all you do:

Visit *www.facthound.com*

Type in this code: 9781491449905

Check out projects, games and lots more at
www.capstonekids.com

CRITICAL THINKING USING THE COMMON CORE

1. What might life be like today for American Indians if the United States had not expanded westward? Support your answer with information from the text and other sources. (Integration of Knowledge and Ideas)

2. The Dakota, Lakota, and Nakota were subjected to repeated broken promises by the U.S. government. How does that history affect the Sioux people today? (Key Ideas and Details)

3. The U.S. government has offered to pay the Great Sioux Nation for wrongfully taking the Black Hills. Why do you think the Sioux want the Black Hills more than the $1 billion owed them? (Integration of Knowledge and Ideas)

INDEX